Is there a conflict between the Law of the Old Testament and the Gospel of the New Testament?

HAS THE LAW BEEN NAILED TO THE CROSS?

Discover the amazing truth from your own Bible...

Mount Ephraim Publishing

www.mountephraimwatchman.org

Has the Law been Nailed to the Cross?

Mount Ephraim Watchman
www.mountephraimwatchman.org

Published by Mount Ephraim Publishing

Printed in the United States of America

1st Edition 2001:
Edited and Arranged by Stephen J. Spykerman
2nd Edition 2004:
Edited and Arranged by Stephen J. Spykerman
3rd Edition 2017:
Edited and Arranged by Eddie R. Rogers

ISBN-13: 978-1544957937
ISBN-10: 1544957939

Front Cover: *Illustration of mural of Moses bringing the Ten Commandments from Mount Sinai taken from original canvas in the Moses Room, House of Lords, Palace of Westminster; London.*

All Scripture references quoted in this booklet are taken from the New King James Bible, unless stated otherwise.

INTRODUCTION

Does the question posed on the front cover of this booklet not appear somewhat irrelevant? Surely, of all the questions that can be asked, this one simply has to be superfluous! Is it not a universally recognized fact within Christian circles that Jesus nailed the law to the cross? What a silly question to ask! Every Christian worth their name knows full well that the Old Testament Law has been done away! This is the one point of doctrine all the hundreds of different Christian denominations in the world are in total agreement on. The many streams of Christianity may disagree with each other on almost any point of doctrine, yet they are in perfect unity on this issue. '*Oh,*' you might exclaim; '*Would that we could have similar unity elsewhere!*' They all agree with one voice that the law has been done away!

Did Jesus not come to usher in the New Covenant? Have we not since the advent of Christ arrived at an altogether new dispensation? Did Jesus not condemn the Scribes and the Pharisees for their hypocrisy and legalism? (Matthew 23:13-15, 23, 25) Were they not so zealous for the law that they forgot all about the spirit and intent of the law? Did Jesus not call them hypocrites and white plastered graves? (Matthew 23:27) Keeping the law certainly did not get the Pharisees in the good books of Jesus, did it? Every true Christian knows the famous words of the Apostle Paul:

"For by grace you have been saved through faith, and that not of yourselves; it is the gift of God, not of works, lest anyone should boast."
(Ephesians 2:8)

All Christian denominations are agreed that '**Grace**' is the key issue. Christians rejoice in the glorious liberty wherewith Christ has set them free and they do not want to become entangled again with the yoke of bondage. (Galatians 5:1) Christians know and they know that they know that righteousness does not come through the keeping of the law. In their view, those wretched people who think that they can gain their salvation through keeping the law are sadly misguided and in bondage to legalism. The Christian walk on the other hand is a walk of faith and their walk is based on the Scripture that says:

"But that no one is justified by the law in the sight of God is evident, for 'the <u>just shall live by faith</u>."
(Galatians 3:11)

Christians are mindful also of the awesome exclamation made by the Apostle Paul in his Letter to the Galatians:

"Christ has redeemed us from the curse of the law, having become a curse for us (for it is written, "Cursed is everyone who hangs on a tree.") " (Galatians 3:13)

Having been delivered through grace and walking the walk of faith, Christians simply do not want to return to the bondage of the law. They have been saved by grace and they do not want to come under the law again.

Having just given the briefest outline of the doctrine that Jesus nailed the law to the cross, I believe it is right for us to examine if this doctrine is true. Most people simply accept the doctrines of their churches without questioning them. However, we should always be willing to ask ourselves the question about any given doctrine: *"Is it true?" When did you last check this particular doctrine about the law having been done away, in your own Bible? Have you ever done it? What if it is wrong? Have you ever seriously researched into any of the doctrines of your church?*

You may well ask why we should challenge what is in effect a universal tenet of the Christian faith? One reason is that it is fair to examine any question of doctrine no matter how strongly held. Any doctrine should be able to stand the test of close examination against the Scriptures. There should never be any no-go areas or sacred cows! The very fact that the many hundreds of different church denominations disagree on almost every single doctrine apart from this one makes me wonder why. Why do all these churches agree on this one doctrine, whilst disagreeing amongst themselves on almost any other? Why are they so united on this particular teaching? What is it about this doctrine that brings such extra ordinary unity? Are you a seeker after truth? Why not find out the answer to this question.

Another most important reason for examining this matter is, because if it is indeed true that the Law has been done away, it does appear to present an apparent contradiction between the Law of the Old Testament and the Gospel of the New Testament. When Church doctrine appears to show up a conflict between the Old Testament and the New Testament, it demands serious investigation. Any true Christian believer worth his salt knows full well that the Bible does not contradict itself. Therefore, if there appears to be a contradiction, we are duty bound to investigate. In this context it really does not matter what the church thinks is true. It also does not matter what you or I think either! The only opinion that counts is God's opinion! Man is simply not qualified to speak on this subject! Only God Himself can tell us whether His Law was abolished at the cross. We find His opinion in His inspired word.

In this booklet we will examine this doctrine and measure it against the word of God. We will concentrate our efforts on the New Testament Scriptures and especially watch out for what Jesus Himself had to say on the subject. It may surprise you to know that Jesus frequently spoke about the law and the commandments. Jesus is the Light of the world and His words will give us the understanding we need. As we look at His words and also at the inspired statements of the Apostles, we will discover that there is a contradiction somewhere along the line. Prepare to be surprised and try to approach the Scriptures with an open mind. Let the Scriptures speak to you rather than your own preconceived ideas. Truth really is stranger than fiction!

NAILED WHAT TO THE CROSS?

There is a Scripture verse in the New Testament that appears to confirm the Christian theory that the Law has been nailed to the cross. We find it in a statement by the Apostle Paul in his letter to the church at Colossae:

> *"Having wiped out the handwriting of requirements that was against us, which was contrary to us. And He has taken it out of the way, having nailed it to the cross."*
> (Colossians 2:14)

Notice, it does not mention here that the Law has been nailed to the cross but rather that '*the handwriting of requirements*' was nailed to the cross. In the Authorized King James Version these '*requirements*' are referred to as '*ordinances*,' which suggests they are of man rather than of God. The Complete Jewish Bible by David Stern refers to these '*requirements*' and '*ordinances*' as being based upon "*man-made rules and teachings*." (Colossians 2:22)

The problem Paul faced with the Colossians was that the pure faith of Jesus and the Apostles was being compromised with legalism and all sorts of rules and regulations to make one more spiritual. The context makes this clear as we see in the subsequent verses where Paul lists some of the things he finds so objectionable. Rules that say; '*do not touch, do not taste, do not handle.*' (Verse 21) In verse 18 he exhorts his followers with the words: "*Let no 'man' beguile you*" and in verse 22 in the New King James Version, Paul speaks about "***the commandments and doctrines of men***," whilst in the next verse he speaks of "***self-imposed religion and false humility***." Clearly, when we look at the context of verse 14 there is no way we can conclude that the Law has been nailed to the cross. Rather Jesus, as our God given Passover Lamb, paid the penalty for our sins and it is our penalty of death that He nailed to the cross. What Jesus did '*wipe out*' on the cross was the complete record of our sin. The blood of Jesus Christ acts as a divine eraser, which erases the record of our sins against us and gives us a clean slate. However, it absolutely does not give us a license to carry on sinning!

HOW DO WE KNOW
WE ARE SAVED?

Most Christians are aware that they are saved by faith and by faith alone. Ask any practicing and committed Christian, *"How do you know you are saved?"* In nine out of ten cases they will quote you, ***"For God so loved the world that He gave His only begotten Son, that whoever believes in Him should not perish but have everlasting life."*** (John 3:16) The question is, can it really be that simple? What kind of faith is the Apostle John talking about? Surely, it has to be the sort of faith that leads to action. The Bible makes it clear that our faith needs to be backed up by deeds, and most serious Christians agree that belief in Jesus alone is not enough. In the Book of James it says, ***"Even the devils also believe, and tremble!"*** (James 2:19) The writer of James then goes on to make the point that, ***"faith without works is dead!"*** Thus, it is all well and good to say that we are saved by grace and faith, yet what is really required is faith that leads to obedience! John makes this very point in verse 36 of the same chapter.

> ***"He who believes in the Son has eternal life; he who does not obey the Son shall not see life, but the wrath of God rests upon him."***
> (John 3:36 Revised Standard Version)

The Living New Testament, the Amplified, as well as the Complete Jewish Bible all refer to this same word *'OBEY.'* If our faith does not lead us to a life of perfect submission and obedience then the wrath of God still rests upon us and we will not inherit or see life.

JESUS WAS NOT A CHRISTIAN!

The Christian Church at large teaches that the Law is done away with and that Jesus has nailed it to the cross. Most Christians have accepted this teaching as the truth and they sincerely believe that this is what the Bible teaches. Few believers ever challenge the beliefs of their churches, as they tend to accept that all the wise theologians, doctors of the law and all the priests and ministers who have gone before could not possibly be wrong. Yet, the question needs to be asked. *Do the Scriptures teach that the Law has been nailed to the cross? Does the Bible teach that the law has been done away with? Are you interested in finding out the truth? What does the Bible really teach?*

One of the biggest handicaps the church labours under is that the church at large has departed from its Hebrew roots. The church has dismissed much of the Old Testament and many of its instructions as being meant for the Jews only. Somehow they seem to forget that their Lord and Saviour was a Jew who kept every point of the law to perfection. He did not just keep the Torah, which means literally, "THE TEACHING" of God but He went beyond that to keep the spiritual intent of the Law/Torah also. Jesus kept God's commandments and He instructed His true disciples with the words:

> **"If you love Me, keep My commandments.**"(John 14:15)

It may well come as a nasty shock to some to know that JESUS **WAS NOT A CHRISTIAN!**

Jesus was a Jew who kept the commandments of God and he faithfully followed all
the precepts of the Torah. By no stretch of the
imagination could Jesus be considered a
Christian and if Christianity had existed in
His day He almost certainly would have criticized it every bit as much as He criticized the
religion of the Pharisees. His disciples believed in His Messiah-ship and they also were
Torah observant Messianic believers. They
too were not Christians!

Jesus in effect said: "**If** you love Me, **if** you '*really*' love
Me, prove it to Me by keeping My commandments!
That is how you demonstrate your love for Me." Talk is
cheap! We demonstrate our love for Him by the extent
to which we are prepared to keep His commandments.
Jesus is speaking to His followers: "*DO AS I DO!*" He
set the example of total obedience to God's word. He
wants His true disciples to be **doers** of the word rather
than **hearers** only. Remember in His day the only
word of God available to mankind was the Old
Testament! The New Testament had not yet been
written. Jesus, the Jewish Saviour of mankind, kept all
the Torah, all the teaching, all the instructions and all
the commandments of the Old Testament. That is the
example He set for His true disciples. He kept the
'quotes un-quotes' "Jewish" Sabbath and also the so-
called "Jewish" Holydays.

His true name was Yeshua, which when one translates
it literally from the Hebrew into English actually means

'SALVATION.' It would be far more appropriate for His followers to call him by His proper Jewish name of Yeshua. At least, if we want to give Him an English name, we should call Him 'Salvation,' which is an accurate translation of His true name and also speaks of His mission here on earth, as He is our 'Salvation.' Jesus is the name given Him by the Greeks and the Romans but it does not have the same meaning and it does not reflect His true name.

This same Yeshua! Jesus spoke to His disciples and said:

> *"He who has My commandments and keeps them, it is he who loves Me. And he who loves Me will be loved by My Father, and I will love him and manifest Myself to him."*
> (John 14:21)

What commandments could He possibly be talking about? The only commandments Yeshua kept were the commandments recorded in the Old Testament. It is the person who keeps these commandments who will be loved by Him and also by the Father. After all, did not the Father give these selfsame commandments to us? What comes to mind is the words Yeshua spoke in His Sermon on the Mount where He's speaking to the assembled multitude, He said:

> *"17 Do not think that I came to destroy the Law (Torah) or the Prophets. I did not come to destroy but to fulfil. 18 For assuredly, I say*

unto you, till heaven and earth pass away, one jot or one tittle will by no means pass from the Law (Torah) till all is fulfilled."
(Matthew 5:17-18)

The Apostle Paul says that: "***Love does no harm to a neighbor, therefore love is the fulfilment of the Law.***" (Romans 13:10). The Law Yeshua referred to is the Law or Torah and the Prophets of the Old Testament, because in His day that is all there was. Did you notice the reference to '*heaven and earth passing away*?' What He in effect is saying is, that until heaven and earth pass away, the Torah teaching and instruction of the Old Testament will apply. As heaven and earth clearly have not passed away yet, we can take it on the authority of Yeshua's inspired Sermon on the Mount that Torah still very much applies today. Yeshua, referring to Torah and the commandments of the Old Testament, goes on to say:

*"19 **Whoever therefore breaks one of the least of these (Old Testament) commandments, and teaches men so, shall be the least in the kingdom of heaven; but whoever does and teaches them, he shall be called great in the kingdom of heaven. 20 For I say to you, that unless your righteousness exceeds the righteousness of the scribes and Pharisees, you will by no means enter the kingdom of heaven.***"*
(Matthew 5:19-20)

The Pharisees got a lot of stick from Messiah because the way some of their leaders were steeped in legalism and hypocrisy. Yet Yeshua nevertheless encourages His disciples to adopt the same diligence of the Pharisees in keeping certain aspects of the Torah:

> *"For you pay tithe of mint and anise and cumin, and have neglected the weightier matters of the law (Torah): justice and mercy and faith. These you ought to have done without leaving the others undone."*
> (Matthew 23:23)

The Pharisees were renowned for keeping the Law of Moses to the finest detail, yet many of them had no conception of the spiritual intent of the law and applied it without any justice, mercy, or faith. Jesus/Yeshua here, whilst pointing to the spiritual intent of the law, is by no means letting them off the hook by allowing them not to keep the law. He in effect is saying:

> *"These (Justice and Mercy and Faith) you ought to have done, without leaving the others (all of Torah) undone."*

THE TRUE TEST OF OUR LOVE

Going back to the Book of John, we find some more extra ordinary statements by the Son of the Living God:

> "*23 If anyone loves Me, he will keep My word; and My Father will love him, and We will come to him and make Our home with him. 24 He who does not love Me does not keep My words; and the word which you hear is not Mine but the Father's who sent Me.*" (John 14:23-24)

Do we begin to see that the TRUE TEST of our love for our Saviour and Redeemer is keeping His commandments? Remember, when He spoke these profound words, there was only one set of commandments written, that is all the commandments written in the Old Testament! Yeshua set the example for us. He kept Torah and He expects His true followers to do the same! Those people who do not keep His commandments simply do not love Him. It does not matter how religious they are. It makes no difference how often they go to church, to Bible study or to prayer meetings. If they do not keep the commandments of God, they do not love Him. This is what the word of God says; the only people who love Him are the ones who keep His commandments.

The Apostle Paul speaks of love as the most important fruit of the Spirit:

> **"But the fruit of the Spirit is love."**
> (Galatians 5:22)

Once Paul has mentioned the most important fruit, he goes on to mention the others:

> **'joy, peace, longsuffering, kindness, goodness, faithfulness, gentleness, self-control'** (Galatians 5:22)

What Paul is saying here, is that if we have that foremost fruit of God's Holy Spirit, our desire will be to keep God's commandments. Remember Yeshua said:

> **"If you love Me, keep My commandments."**

We demonstrate the love of God in us by keeping His commandments and as we do so a blessing comes upon us. Part of that blessing comes to us through the other fruits of the Spirit such as joy and peace. As a direct consequence of our obedience and submission to God's Law and His commandments, we come to understand the very nature and character of God. Through His Spirit, God then progressively starts to transform our character and we acquire the other fruits of His Spirit such as longsuffering, kindness, goodness, faithfulness, gentleness and self-control. The point is that when we start to live in obedience to God's commandments, we effectively are living according to God's own standards and once we begin to do that the Spirit of the living God starts to impart His divine nature in us. The essence of the divine nature is love, joy, peace, longsuffering, kindness, goodness, faithfulness, gentleness and self-control. Thus, as we walk in obedience to His commandments we ultimately become like Him.

HOW TO ABIDE IN HIS LOVE

The Scriptures speak of *'abiding in His love.'* What is the meaning of the word *'abide?'* What does it mean to *'abide in His love?'* To abide means to *'act in accordance with'* or *'remain faithful to'* or it can mean *'to remain, continue in'* or *'to dwell in'* and it can also mean *'to endure'* or *'to persevere with.'* Yeshua is in effect giving us a clear definition of who His true disciples are. His true disciples *'abide'* in Him by *'acting'* in accordance with His word. They *'abide'* in Him by remaining faithful to it and they *'abide'* in Him by enduring whatever consequences their obedience to His word brings and they *'abide'* in Him by persevering regardless. His true disciples keep His commandments! We said that His true disciples will measure their beliefs and preconceptions and ideas against the word of God in the Bible and if they find any conflict they will follow God's word rather than their own opinions or the opinions of their church or denomination.

For these people the only opinion that counts is God's opinion as expressed in His word. In other words, they are prepared to submit their lives to the word of God and make changes where necessary, no matter what it costs. We have the cast iron promise from Messiah Yeshua that when we truly abide in His word with all that this entails, we will come to know the truth. The knowledge of the truth, as we apply it in our lives, will then set us free. **Truth comes to us through our obedience!** The plain fact is that what we know and what we understand is often not the truth. Most of us on our life's journey have picked up a whole lot of error. As we come to learn God's standards, we have to unlearn our own standards and preconceived ideas. Our own standards are usually the standards of the world, yet the true disciples of Yeshua are called to come out of this world. It is only those who are prepared to measure what they know and understand against the ultimate yardstick of God's word in the Bible, with a completely open and submissive mind, who comes to know the truth. Then, it is only those few who are prepared to obey and walk in that truth that will be set free. Only those few exceptional individuals who are prepared to jettison their false beliefs and erroneous preconceptions in the light of the Scriptures can become Yeshua's true disciples.

Why am I going through this material? The simple reason is because Yeshua speaks about His true disciples '*abiding*' in Him. First of all, He refers to Himself as '**THE TRUE VINE**' and He then goes on to say the following:

> "*4 Abide in Me, and I in you. As the branch cannot bear fruit of itself, unless it abide in the vine, neither can you, unless you abide in Me. 5 I am the vine, you are the branches, He who abides in Me, and I in him,*

bears much fruit; for without Me you can do nothing." (John 15:4-5)

THE QUESTION IS:

"HOW DO WE ABIDE IN HIM?"

Let Yeshua Himself give the answer. Let the inspired word of God give you the answer!

THIS IS HOW!

> *"If you keep My commandments, you will abide in My love, just as I have kept My Fathers commandments and abide in His love."*
>
> (John 15:10)

DOES THIS NOT MAKE IT CRYSTAL CLEAR?

Yeshua kept His Father's commandments and He expects His disciples to follow His good example!

Another thought on this subject is this; If Jesus/Yeshua represents the vine that is faithfully keeping His Fathers commandments, how can you have the branches of that same vine not keeping the commandments? On the one hand, you have the vine keeping the commandments of God and on the other hand you have the branches of that same vine not keeping the commandments of God. Does this make sense to you? It goes against the laws of nature itself. You can ask any horticulturalist or gardener! You cannot have a vine doing

---

one thing and the branches of that same vine doing something completely different!

This is really a most serious issue as Jesus makes it plain that His Father is the vinedresser and He goes on to say:

> *"1 I am the true vine, and My Father is the vinedresser. 2 Every branch in Me that does not bear fruit He takes away; and every branch that bears fruit He prunes, that it may bear more fruit."* (John 15:1-2)

Yeshua really spells it out here and He is in fact saying that if we do not keep the commandments, that not only will we not abide in His love but also that His Father will actually remove us from the vine itself! In verse six of the same chapter, He confirms that we will be removed from the vine if we do not keep the commandments. This is what He says:

> *"If anyone does not abide in Me, he is cast out as a branch and is withered; and they gather them and throw them into the fire, and they are burned."* (John 15:6)

This surely is strong language coming from Jesus but then Jesus, the Son of the living God cannot tolerate sin.

DEFINITION OF SIN

This leads us to our next point. Most Christians do not know what sin is! This may seem a highly provocative statement to you but nonetheless, I am sad to say, it is absolutely true. If you were to carry out a poll in your church, you will find that very few Christians are able to define exactly what sin is. In all probability even the pastor, minister, vicar or priest himself would not be able to give you a biblically correct answer. What then is sin? The inspired word of the Bible makes it quite clear and it gives us a most precise definition.

> *"Whoever committeth sin trans-*
> *gresseth also the law: FOR SIN IS*
> *THE TRANSGRESSION OF THE*
> *LAW."* (1 John 3:4 KJV)

There you have it from the word of God! Does this not make a mockery of the church's stance that the Law is done away with and that Jesus nailed it to the cross? If this were true that would mean that no one was able to sin anymore, as if there is no more Law to be transgressed there can also be no more sin. On the cross Jesus paid the penalty for our sins but He most certainly did not abolish the Law of His Father in heaven. Let's discover what else the Apostle John has to say on the subject:

> *"3 Now by this we know that we*
> *know Him, if we keep His com-*
> *mandments. 4 He who says, "I know*
> *Him," and does not keep His com-*

mandments, is a liar, and the truth is not in him." (1 John 2:3-4)

The Apostle does not mince his words, does he? He is definitely not being politically correct here. This is really powerful stuff! What an awesome statement this is! The Apostle tells us here that if we do not keep His (God's) commandments (Torah), we simply do not belong to God. **If we say that we know Jesus and yet we do not keep His commandments, God's word says we are liars!** This is plain speaking! Could it really be any clearer? Some might try to defend themselves by saying that the commandments of Jesus were different from the commandments of God. Surely, this cannot have any credibility at all. Does the Bible reveal that Yeshua, the Son of the living God, rebelled against His own Father in heaven by disobeying His commandments? If He had done so, you and I would still be in our sins, as He would not have qualified to be the Saviour of the world.

Either you accept the Torah and Yeshua, [Christ Jesus], or you reject both the Torah and Yeshua, just listen to Yeshua's own instruction:

> "46 **For if you believed Moses, you would believe Me, for he wrote about Me. 47 But if you do not believe his writings, how will you believe My words?**" (John 5:46-47)

WALK JUST AS HE WALKED

The Apostle John goes on to say:

> "*5 But whoever keeps His word, truly the love of God is perfected in him. By this we know that we are in Him. 6 He who says he abides in Him ought Himself also to walk just as He walked.*" (1 John 2:5-6)

John here in effect is saying that keeping the commandments of God leads to the love of God being perfected in us. If we say that Messiah Yeshua (Jesus Christ) abides in us, then we are to walk just AS HE WALKED, in perfect obedience to His Father. How do we know that? The scriptures are very clear on this.

Paul, having just emphasised God's Law by quoting the tenth commandment, goes on to say:

> "*Therefore THE LAW IS HOLY, and the commandment holy and just and good.*" (Romans 7:12)

Then in verse 14 he says:

> "*For we know that THE LAW IS SPIRITUAL, but I am carnal, sold under sin.*" (Romans 7:14)

YOU ARE NOT UNDER THE LAW BUT UNDER GRACE

In the Garden of Eden Adam and Eve were being offered a simple choice by God. The choice was between the Tree of Life and the Tree of the Knowledge of Good and Evil. These trees were symbolical of two ways of life that were completely opposite to each other. They were instructed that they could eat of every tree in the garden and this included the fruit from the Tree of Life. Had they chosen to eat of this tree it would have brought them untold physical as well as spiritual blessings. The Tree of Life, as the name implies would have given them life eternal. God had clearly spelt out the consequences for making the wrong choice. Both Adam and Eve knew full well that God had said that if they ate of the Tree of Knowledge that they would surely die. They knew that one choice meant life and that the other meant death. It was made very clear to them. We all know the story of what choice they made. They made the same choice that every man, woman or child has made ever since. They did their own thing! It is natural for man to always want to do his own thing. This is the human condition. Humans naturally do not want to go God's way. Invariably, they want to go their own way. We all know this is true from our own experience as well as from the experience of our children. The choice of the Tree of Life versus the Tree of the Knowledge of Good and Evil has never gone away. Even Moses when exhorting the children of Israel to keep the commandments of God knew full well that they would fail. In his final testament to the tribes of Israel, he placed before them the same choice God had put before Adam and Eve.

> *"I call heaven and earth as witnesses today against you, that I have set before you life and death, blessing and cursing; therefore choose life, that both you and your descendants may live."*
>
> (Deuteronomy 30:19)

The whole story of the Old Testament is the account of how the Israelites failed time and again to stay on the right course. The world at large has failed to choose *'life'* in an even bigger way. It is true to say that once we start to measure by God's own standards the whole world has failed and man is a failure before God. As we have already seen on the previous page, the Apostle Paul pointed out that:

> *"...we would not have known sin except through the law."*
>
> (Romans 7:7)

This statement infers that the Law (Torah) came into play to *'highlight'* the sinfulness of sin. The Law was introduced to show the people how bad they were. It was introduced to show mankind that they did not measure up to God's standards. Torah or the Law was instituted by God to make sin exceedingly sinful. The Law is the yardstick by which we can measure our life against the standards of God Himself. The Law is a gauge by which we can measure the sinfulness of our character. This is why the apostle Paul exhorted his fellow disciples to do as follows:

> **"Therefore do not let sin reign in your mortal body, that you should obey its lusts.**" (Romans 6:12)

Paul says that we must not allow sin to rule in our bodies. Sin is the transgression of the Law. Paul decidedly is not saying that we should get rid of the Law and make out that it does not exist or that it does not apply anymore. He is saying exactly the opposite. Paul says here that we must not allow sin or the transgression of the Law to rule in our mortal bodies, so that it makes you obey its desires. He then goes on to point out the reason why, by saying:

> **"For sin shall not have dominion over you, for you are not under the law (legalism) but under grace.**"
> (Romans 6:14)

Now why is **Paul saying to the disciples that they are not under the Law?** We need to understand the background Paul came from. He was brought up in Torah. He was an eminent scholar and pupil of the great Gamaliel. He was a Rabbi and teacher of the Law. All of a sudden he says that we are not under the Law but that we are under grace! What does he mean? The distinction is quite simple really. Paul has become aware that humanly none of us are capable of keeping the Law. It just is not in us to do so. We are simply incapable of obeying the just requirements of God's Law. No human being can live up to the perfect standards of God's Law. We are totally inadequate within ourselves to obey the just demands of Torah. THAT MEANS YOU ARE UNDER THE LAW! You are under it!

You are under its curse, you are under its oppression and you are under its penalty! The Law has become much like the '*Sword of Damocles*' hanging over you. It has become a threat to you. It has become a threat simply because there is no way that you can fulfil its just requirements. That is the reason! That is why it ends up as legalism. If you are going through the motions to keep the Law, knowing full well that you are certain to fall short, then it becomes mere legalism. If you are living by a set of rules that you cannot abide by, the consequences of your failure will hang over you because you know there really is no solution. Paul as a Torah observant Rabbi had experienced this. He had all his life with all his heart and with all his might tried to obey Torah and yet he had failed. He knew the Torah off by heart and yet he failed to keep it to the standards that God in His perfect righteousness demanded. As a Jew and as a Rabbi, he had every advantage and yet he failed. He was one of those rare people who could see the equation. He could understand how something as perfect and as beautiful as Torah could become a threat to you. He could understand how it could become oppression to you, as no one is able to keep the just requirements of God's holy, righteous and spiritual Law. Thus, you were always going to be disappointed. You were always going to be under its condemnation. Something that should be your friend has thus become something that would condemn you. That is why the apostle says; "**You are not under the law but you are under grace.**"

WHAT DOES GRACE MEAN?

Literally, it means '*unmerited pardon.*' The spiritual meaning contains a reference to your condition. If you are '*under grace*' you have been empowered by the Holy Spirit, (the Spirit of God) inside of you to attain unto salvation and eternal life. That is the '*grace*' you have received because you did not deserve it. You came into the sacrifice of Jesus (Yeshua), who died on your behalf and who paid the penalty for your sins. He also paid the price for Adam's failure to make the right choice in the first place. Thus, you came into a condition of '*grace,*' which you did not deserve because, as a serial sinner all you deserve is death! The Scripture makes it quite clear that this is what we all deserve; "**as there is none righteous no not one!**"

So, you are in a condition of God's '*grace*' having received the power of the Holy Spirit to impart in you the righteousness of God that would enable you to keep the Torah/Law. It is because you have received the Spirit of God that you are now able to fulfil the just requirements of the Law. For the first time in your life, you can fulfil the just requirements of the law, so that you no longer have to live '*UNDER*' it but instead, you can now live '*IN*' it. That's the difference! **Grace enables you to live within the Law!** It is because of that same '*grace*' that you come to love the Law and the commandments of God. You are able to live '*within*' the

Law, as the Spirit of God within you enables you, not only to keep the Law but also to fulfil the spiritual intent behind the Law. Thus, it is indeed '*BY GRACE*' that the true disciple of Jesus/Yeshua is able to walk in perfect obedience to the Law. This is not legalism! This is nothing other than a demonstration of true love. Again, I quote those immortal words of Jesus: "***If you love Me, keep My commandments!***" Once empowered by the Spirit of God within you, you are keeping His commandments simply because you love Him. You do not do it out of fear or because you feel you have to. You do not do it out of a misguided belief that keeping the commandments is somehow going to earn you your salvation. Absolutely not! You are keeping the commandments simply because you love your Saviour and Redeemer. In your obedience, you are declaring your love for your Master and Lord. You obey Him because you love Him and that is all there is to it.

CAN YOU LOVE JESUS AND HATE THE LAW OF HIS FATHER?

We have just looked into the word of God. We have covered no less than 25 Scriptures from the New Testament. Hopefully, God has spoken to you with His voice of authority. Could any of this be any clearer? I have deliberately quoted God's word primarily from the New Testament to give the word extra emphasis. Many Christians believe that the New Testament speaks of the Law having been done away. They maintain that the church does not need to keep the commandments of

God because they believe that Jesus has nailed them to the cross.

From the 25 Scriptures we have just covered, I personally find it hard to believe how the church could possibly have come to this conclusion. Satan the ultimate rebel and lawbreaker is an arch-deceiver and he has put his spirit of rebellion into the church. Satan hates the Law of God. He also hates anyone who walks with God by observing His Law. Satan is the god of this world and in his world, keeping the commandments of God is not a popular activity. Satan has distilled his spirit into the world and the world hates the Law of God. The apostle Paul makes this point very well:

> *"The carnal mind is enmity against God; for it is not subject to the law of God, nor indeed can be."*
> (Romans 8:7)

Can you see what the Apostle Paul is saying? He clearly explains that the carnal or the natural fleshly mind of man hates God. WHY? Paul answers the question:

> **'Because it is not subject to the law of God!'**

The reverse side of this equation is that if only man would be subject to God's Law, man would love God. The history of the Jews is a case in point. Satan's hatred for the Law of God makes him hate every Torah observant Jew. That is why the Jews throughout their history have always been persecuted by the world. They have been the odd ones out. They have always stood out like a sore thumb. Their insistence in keeping the commandments of God has been a continuing thorn in Satan's side and that is why he has always wanted to wipe them out. In the past, he has used the Christian church to great effect as his instrument in being a special scourge to the Jews. The church has persecuted them through murderous crusades, pogroms, inquisitions and expulsions, as well as through the ultimate horror of the Holocaust. Today, Satan is using Islam to try to root out the Jews and expunge them from the face of the earth with much of the Christian church giving them their support and encouragement. Satan hates the Law of God and he has instilled this hatred into the hearts of men. Here lies the answer to the question I posed right at the beginning. This is the reason for the extraordinary unity amongst all of the numerous Christian denominations. They disagree among themselves on almost any subject or doctrine, yet when it comes to their doctrine on the Law having been abolished they speak with one voice! This fact alone should make one suspicious. Their voice is none other than the voice of Satan the arch-deceiver and prince of rebellion who hates the Law of God! It is because of this hatred that the Church is saying that the Law is done away!

Consider also that Jesus was an Orthodox Torah observant Jew who kept the Law of God in every detail. Consider that He never once sinned; that He throughout His life kept all of the commandments of God with a perfect heart. If the Jew, Jesus, was to come again in His first guise as the suffering servant, keeping all of the commandments of God as the spotless Lamb of God, exhorting all of His followers to obey the Law, I am utterly convinced that the Christian church would crucify and murder Him afresh. Why do I say this? Simply, because the Christian church hates the Law of God! What a contradiction! The Church that professes to love Jesus hates Torah, the Law of His Father! What an amazing contradiction! We need to examine our own hearts in this area and remember the words of Paul who said that the Law is Holy as well as Spiritual.

THE WHEAT AND THE TARES

Most Christians are familiar with the parable of the Wheat and the Tares, which Jesus used as an analogy of His kingdom. The account is about a man who sowed good seed in his field and then late at night whilst he was asleep, an enemy came and sowed bad seed or tares in that same field. The enemy wanted to wreck the harvest because he hated the owner of the field. When the grain appeared, the labourers noticed that the grain was almost smothered by tares or weeds. They questioned their master about the quality of the seed he had sown and they were told that an enemy had gone out of his way to deliberately spoil the harvest. The labourers then wanted to clear the field of those wretched tares that were so badly affecting the crop but their master told them to leave well enough alone until the time of the harvest. The owner of the field was concerned that if the tares were pulled up at this stage, it might possibly do damage to his precious wheat. When the time of the harvest came the reapers were told to first collect the tares in bundles ready for burning, and to then collect the wheat to be placed in the barn.

After Jesus had related this parable to the multitude, His disciples asked Him privately what message He was trying to get across to the people. They asked Him to explain the meaning of the parable. This is how Jesus answered them:

> "37 *He who sows the good seed is the Son of Man.* 38 *The field is the world, the good seeds are the sons of the kingdom, but the bad seeds are the sons of the wicked one.* 39 *The enemy who sowed them is the devil, the harvest is the end of the age, and the reapers are the angels.*" (Matthew 13:37–39)

Here we have the whole kingdom message that Jesus came to preach in a nutshell. It is He who sows the good seed that leads to obedience and conversely, it is the devil that sows the bad seed that leads to disobedience or lawlessness. Now let us see what happens to those lawless ones:

> "41 *The Son of Man will send out His angels, and they will gather out of His kingdom all things that offend, and those who practice lawless-ness,* 42 *and will cast them into a furnace of fire. There will be wailing and gnashing of teeth.*"
> (Matthew 13:41-42)

The dictionary describes a tare as *'an injurious weed resembling wheat when young.'* Here in this Scripture Jesus gives His disciples His own definition of what a tare truly is. To summarise His words; **"A tare is an offensive, good for nothing, and lawless weed that is only good for burning that most definitely will not be allowed into His kingdom!"** Notice also that as His angels collect these lawless tares, they will be *'wailing and gnashing their teeth.'* The reason why people will wail and gnash their teeth in anger and utter frustration is because all the while these tares were growing up in God's field they actually thought they were wheat! All their lives they thought they were the righteous ones. They thought that because they were *"saved by grace"* they therefore, did not have to keep the Law or the commandments. They thought the Law had been done away with. They had assumed that it had been nailed to the cross. Jesus concludes His parable with a final warning:

> ***"He who has ears to hear, let him hear!"*** (Matthew 11:15)

SUMMARY

We have seen that the Jesus that the Christian Church worships was in fact a Torah observant Jew. He was not only a Jew but He was a Rabbi (Teacher of the Law) as well, with His own group of dedicated disciples.

- This same Jesus/Yeshua set the parameters for us as to how to demonstrate our love for Him. He said: *"If you love Me, keep My commandments."* He Himself kept the Torah which are the teachings, instructions and commandments of the God of Israel and He said to His disciples: *"DO AS I DO,"* follow My example!

- He clearly indicated that He had not come to destroy the Law, by saying that not one jot or one tittle would be taken away. Logic tells us that if He had not come to destroy it, He could not possibly have nailed it to His cross later on!

- He also went on to say that anyone who really loved Him would keep His commandments. We established that the very first fruit of the Spirit is love. He loved His Father by keeping His Commandments and His true disciples likewise, demonstrated their love for Him through their obedience to His commandments.

- Yeshua went on to show His followers that the only way they could '*abide*' in Him would be through the keeping of His commandments.

- We then looked at the most authoritative definition of what sin is and established that **"sin is the transgression of God's Law!"** Any Christian knows that we are saved by grace but surely that grace can never be a license to sin? It can never be a license to break God's Law!

- Then there was that shocking statement by the Apostle John where he indicated that anyone who says that they '*know*' Jesus and yet does not keep the commandments is a liar!

- The same Apostle then went on to say that when we keep the commandments of God, we have the love of God perfected in us. Surely, this is something we should all desire?

- We then established from the Scriptures that Yeshua "*knew no sin*," was "*without sin*" and was "*separate from sinners*."

- From there we saw how the Apostle James instructed us to "*keep the whole Law*," whilst pointing out to us that if we stumble even in one point of the Law, we are guilty of breaking all the commandments.

- We noted the words of the Apostle Paul who told us that as, **"the wages of sin is death**," we should not serve or become slaves to sin."

- He also made the point that we would not have known sin except through the Law and he emphasised that the **Law was Holy and Spiritual**.

- We saw that being saved by grace means that you have obtained the power to live within the Law. For the first time in your life, you can fulfil the just requirements of the Law, so that you no longer have to live '*UNDER*' it but instead you can now live '*IN*' it. That's the difference! **Grace enables you to live within the law!**

- Finally, we saw that Jesus in the parable of the wheat and the tares described the tares as lawless weeds that were not walking in obedience to His Fathers commandments. We noticed that they offended Him and that at the time of the harvest, He instructed His angels to reap them and collect them for burning.

Now tell me, how on earth can the Church maintain, after all these statements to the contrary by Jesus Himself, as well as by the Apostle's John, James and Paul, that the Law has been done away?

Conclusion: This Christian doctrine plainly cannot be based on the Scriptures, which are the revealed word of God. There can thus be only one answer; their doctrine is a doctrine of demons. When you think about this, the consequences are really very serious.

THE MOST TERRIBLE WORDS IN THE NEW TESTAMENT

It is a strange quirk of human nature that whenever we read any words of rebuke in the Bible that we seem to suffer from an inbuilt reluctance to apply those words to ourselves. Somehow, it is always the other fellow, never us! Yet, the truth is that more often than not the words of correction and rebuke apply to us. I have often wondered about the words of Jesus in His Sermon on the Mount, which must surely rank amongst the most sobering words in the whole Bible.

> *"Not everyone who says to Me, 'Lord. Lord,' shall enter the kingdom of heaven, but HE WHO DOES THE WILL OF MY FATHER IN HEAVEN. Many will say to Me in that day, 'Lord, Lord, have we not prophesied in Your name, cast out demons in Your name, and done many wonders in Your name?' And then I will declare to them, 'I NEVER KNEW YOU; depart from Me, YOU WHO PRACTICE LAW – LESS - NESS."* (Mathew 7:21-23)

Can you see it? Did you notice what He said? It is only those who **DO THE WILL OF HIS FATHER IN HEAVEN** that will enter into His kingdom! Even though they thought that they had lived a life of service to Him, prophesying and casting out demons in His name, as well as doing many wonders, it apparently has all been for nothing! Their own Jesus says to them: *"I don't know you — get out and leave Me -you who PRACTICE LAWLESSNESS!"* Lawless people are those who consistently disobey the Law of God. Does this not make it clear as a bell that Yeshua is talking about people who believe in Him and say that they are following Him but who will not submit themselves to keeping His commandments? They practice lawlessness instead.

It is this spirit of lawlessness inside the Christian Church — the spirit that says that the Law has been done away, that is the spirit of Anti-Christ.

ARE YOU PRACTISING LAWLESSNESS?

Even in the days of the early church the Apostle Paul was warning that the anti-Christ spirit was already at work. You can be sure that Satan is always on the job — he is a spirit being of awesome power and he does not need holidays. Just look at these words of the Apostle Paul:

> *"7 For the mystery of lawlessness is already at work; only He who now restrains will do so until He is taken out of the way. 8 And then the lawless one will be revealed, whom the Lord will consume with the breath of His mouth and destroy with the brightness of His coming. 9*

The coming of the lawless one is according to the working of Satan, with all power, signs and lying wonders, 10 and with all unrighteous deception among those who perish, because they did not receive the love of the truth, that they might be saved. 11 And for this reason God will send them strong delusion, that they should believe the lie, 12 that they might all be condemned who did not believe the truth but had pleasure in unrighteousness." (2 Thessalonians 2:7-12)

The strong delusion and the lie the Christian church has swallowed hook line and sinker is the lie that the Law has been nailed to the cross. It is this lie that will separate them from the vine and keep them outside the Kingdom of God. It is because they have followed this satanic lie that Jesus will refuse them entry into His Kingdom with these terrible words: "*I never knew you; Depart from Me you who practice lawlessness!*"

THE EARLY CHURCH KEPT THE COMMANDMENTS

I need to emphasise the keeping of the commandments in the context of studying the Bible and understanding the Scriptures. The reason is that there is a lot the church does not and cannot see or understand about the Scriptures, simply because it does not walk in obedience to the commandments! The church teaches contrary to the words of Jesus, that the Law is done away with. **The Christian church has been deceived in this matter and it believes in a lie**.

The reason why I have especially emphasised the words of Yeshua (Jesus) about the importance of keeping the commandments is because disobedience causes you to become spiritually blind. It is an undisputed fact of history that the early church did keep all of the commandments. All the apostles and early disciples like their Master Yeshua were Torah observant Jews, who kept the Sabbath and God's Holydays, as mentioned in Leviticus 23. The truth is that Rome, which from the very beginning had slaughtered and martyred the early followers of Christ, declared itself a Christian Empire under Emperor Constantine and thus, she effectively hijacked the church Jesus had founded. All traces of the Jewish origins of the church were subsequently erased through the most brutal persecution of the true believers. After three to four centuries of this process a wholly new church emerged that had adopted many of the pagan customs of Rome and its conquered territories and the world entered a period that subsequently became known as the '*Dark Ages.*' The Christian church we see today still carries much of that pagan baggage, despite the efforts of the great reformers during the Reformation. Thus, the church has departed from its original Hebrew roots and it has departed from the ancient paths laid down in the Old Testament. This is a most important historical fact, which cannot be emphasised enough, as without understanding the Jewish roots of our faith it is well-nigh impossible to arrive at the truth. If you are a genuine seeker after truth, then you need to return to the faith of the Patriarchs and the Prophets, which was the same faith Yeshua and the early church walked in.

I CHANGE NOT!

The Prophet Isaiah has some beautifully poetic words to say about the unchanging nature of God's word.

> *"The grass withers, the flower*
> *fades, but the word of our God*
> *stands forever."* (Isaiah 40:8)

There absolutely cannot and may not be any conflict between the Law of God in the Old Testament and the Gospels of the New Testament. We have looked at the words of Jesus and some of His Apostles on the subject, which conclusively prove that there really is no conflict at all. The New Testament Apostle James, writing in his Book of James gives the most magnificent accolade to the Law of God:

> *"If you really fulfil the 'royal law'*
> *according to the Scripture, 'You*

***shall love your neighbour as
yourself, 'you do well.'*** " (James 2:8)

The Law of the Old Testament is also the Law of the
New Testament and as we have just seen, it is referred
to as THE ROYAL LAW. Can it really be credible that
this commandment, to love our neighbour, as we love
ourselves, has been nailed to the cross? Just think,
where is the sense in all of this? Does this mean we are
not obliged to love our neighbour anymore and we can
be as mean and nasty to him as we like? Are we allowed
to hate, to lie, steal and murder now? Are we allowed to
curse God, worship idols and commit adultery, now
that the Law has been nailed to the cross? Where is the
logic in this Christian doctrine? Where is the Scriptural
justification for it? Here we have a New Testament
writer calling upon us to fulfil the *'Royal Law,'* whilst
clearly referring to the commandments of God. There
obviously is no conflict in the mind of the Apostle
James! The *'Royal Law'* of God's commandments is as
valid in the New Testament as it ever was in the Old
Testament. Then to cap it all, we need to especially
consider the revelation of the Prophet Malachi, who
speaking about the essential nature of God, tells us the
following:

> "***For I am the Lord, I CHANGE
> NOT.***" (Malachi 3:6 KJV)

God says here, speaking with absolute sovereign
authority through His Prophet Malachi; '**I CHANGE
NOT!**' We have also seen how the *'Word of the Lord,'*
as enshrined in His *'royal law,'* stands forever. If God
Himself does not change, why on earth should He

change His immutable Law, which is such a perfect reflection of His holy righteous character? Why should He go against His own very nature? Why should He change the Laws that reflect His own standards? **Why should He change the very commandments that He designed to do us good and to bless us?** Why, why, and why? You tell me why should He do such a thing?

TRADITION VERSUS TRUTH

Having come this far, I dare say many of you have been horrified to discover that for most of your life you have believed in a lie. Some of you may well be in a state of shock, whilst others may be in a state of denial and unbelief. The hardest thing for any person to do is to admit that you have been wrong. To admit that you have been wrong all your life is even harder.

The Christian Church in teaching that the Law of God has been nailed to the cross has made the same mistake, as did the Pharisees in the time of Jesus, only in reverse. The Pharisees in the days of Jesus were the established order, much as today the mainline Christian churches are accepted as the established order. The Pharisees were obsessed with keeping every miniscule detail of the Law, yet failed to practice the spiritual intent of the Law. Yet the focus of the Christian Church on the other hand is almost entirely on the things of the spirit, whilst declaring that the Law has been abolished. One keeps the Law and ignores the spirit; the other does not keep the Law and accepts the spirit. Having brought it down to its simplest form, it is easy to see that both the Pharisees and Christianity represent two sides of the same coin. Now we all know from the words in the New Testament that Jesus was not very complimentary about the Pharisees. You can be sure that Jesus today would be just as scathing about Christians as He was then about the Pharisees. It was adherence to their wretched traditions that was the undoing of the Pharisees. The Christian Church is in exactly the same boat, as it is the traditions of the church that have led them astray. Let us just check the Scriptures and see what Jesus/Yeshua has to say about the subject:

> *"Why do you also transgress the commandment of God because of your tradition?"* (Matthew 15:3)

What a good question! Is this not exactly what the Church has done? He goes on to say in verse 6:

> *"Thus you have made the commandments of God of no effect by your tradition."* (Matthew 15:6)

Although Jesus was addressing the Pharisees then, He is today addressing Christians with the same words. He is addressing the wicked Christian tradition that the commandments of God have been abolished. It is by this tradition that they have at a stroke, made the commandments of God of no effect! He then goes on to rebuke the Church today by recalling the words of the Prophet Isaiah:

> *"Hypocrites! Well did Isaiah prophesy about you, saying: 'These*

people draw near to Me with their mouth, and honour Me with their lips, but their heart is far from Me. And in vain they worship Me, teaching as doctrines the commandments of men." (Matthew 15:7-9)

Any Christian reading this would automatically assume that Jesus is speaking about the Pharisees. It seems more likely He is addressing the Christian believer of today. It is the Christian who is the Pharisee today, as he teaches as doctrines the commandments of men. He wilfully rejects the spiritual and holy commandments of God by stating that they have been done away. Thus, such a Christian draws near to Jesus with his mouth and honours Him with his lips but his heart is far from Christ and he worships Him altogether in vain. What a terrible indictment this truly is!

Can we imagine what it means to worship Him in vain? We have already considered those terrifying words of Jesus, where He says that He does not '*know*' you. He does not '*know*' those Christians, because He simply cannot have fellowship with people who do not keep His Fathers commandments. He cannot have fellowship with lawlessness.

ARE YOU WEARING THE WRONG GARMENT TO THE WEDDING?

Do you remember the parable of the wedding feast in Matthew 22? How Jesus described the kingdom of heaven as being like a king inviting lots of people to come to the wedding of his son? Sadly, all the invitations were declined. People made their excuses some more flimsy than others and they showed no respect to the king or his son. Some even mistreated the king's servants and killed a number of them. The king was furious and punished those wrongdoers. He then told his servants to go into the highways to invite new guests both bad and good. Once the wedding hall was filled the parable goes on to say:

> *"11 **But when the king came in to see the guests, he saw a man there who did not have on a wedding garment. 12 So he said to him, 'Friend, how did you come in here without a wedding garment?' And he was speechless. 13 Then the king said to the servants, 'Bind him hand and foot, take him away, and cast him into outer darkness; there will be weeping and gnashing teeth.' 14 For many are called, but few are chosen**."* (Matthew 22:11-14)

Notice, the man was speechless! He just did not have an answer as to why he was wearing the wrong garment. You can tell by his reaction to the king's question that the man immediately knew what the king meant by a wedding garment. Yet, before the king had singled him out, he had been unaware that he was wearing the wrong clothes for this wedding. Once the king had confronted him, he knew there was no excuse. Can you imagine the man's embarrassment in front of all those guests? So, what does it all mean? The king clearly represents God the Father, whereas his son symbolises Jesus/Yeshua the Messiah. The wedding feast can only refer to the marriage feast of the Lamb spoken of in the Book of Revelation.

> *"7 Let us be glad and rejoice and give Him glory, for the marriage feast of the Lamb has come, and His wife has made herself ready. 8 And to her it was granted to be arrayed in fine linen, clean and bright, for the fine linen is the righteous acts of the saints. 9 Then he said to me, 'Write: Blessed are those who are called to the marriage supper of the Lamb!'"* (Revelation 19:7-9)

From the above, we can see that those invited to the marriage feast were dressed in fine linen, which symbolised the righteous lifestyle they had followed. Here then, we see the wedding garment identified as fine linen. After the marriage supper of the Lamb, we witness His righteous saints following their glorious KING OF KINGS AND LORD OF LORDS on white horses.

"And the armies in heaven, clothed in fine linen, white and clean, followed him on white horses."
(Revelation 19:14)

Notice, how special emphasis is placed on the fine linen garments being both white and clean which denotes the sinless condition of those righteous saints. We have already established from 1 John 3:4 that **"sin is the transgression of the Law!"** Therefore, if we are to wear the correct garment to the King's wedding feast for His Son, we need to dress in white linen representing our righteousness in Him.

This is beautifully expressed in:

"He made Him who knew no sin to be sin for us, so that we might become the righteousness of God in Him." (2 Corinthians 5:21)

The Apostle Paul then exhorts the true *'called out'* disciples of Jesus as follows:

"Do not be unequally yoked together with unbelievers. For what fellowship has righteousness with lawlessness? And what communication has light with darkness?"
(2 Corinthians 6:14)

Do we get the picture? The correct wedding garment is worn by the person who has lived a righteous life of obedience to God's Law. The only guests to the King's wedding feast wearing those fine linen garments are those who without exception have lived a life of willing obedience to God's commandments. They have qualified to be there because they have lived by God's own standards and rejected the lawless ways of this world. These righteous saints have not accepted the doctrine of lawlessness, which erroneously states that Jesus/Yeshua, the Son of the Living God, nailed the Law of His Father to the Cross! The fine linen garments, white and clean are symbolic of their spiritual condition. This is why the man caught out by the king not wearing the correct wedding garment became utterly speechless. The king in fact confronted him with his lawless life and he knew immediately he did not belong. True Torah discipleship is found in righteous action. It is only those who have kept the commandments of God who qualify for an invitation to that greatest banquet of all time — the marriage feast of the Lamb.

A PATRIARCHAL
GENERATION GAP

In the last book of the Old Testament there is an amazing statement that has many people puzzled, as it is speaking about a generation gap, which is going to take Elijah the prophet to mend and bridge. Let us see what it says:

> *"5 Behold, I will send you Elijah before the coming of the great and dreadful day of the LORD. 6 And he will turn the hearts of the fathers to the children, and the hearts of the children to their fathers, lest I come and strike the earth with a curse."*
> (Malachi 4:5-6)

Who are these fathers being referred to here? Who are the children? Quite simply, the fathers are the patriarchs of Israel and the children are their offspring! This prophecy is intended for the time immediately ahead of us, as we know it to be *"that great and dreadful day of the LORD"* has not yet come. The problem being addressed here is that a major estrangement has developed in the hearts of Abraham, Isaac and Jacob, the fathers of Israel and the hearts of the children of Israel. What-is-more, it is going to take the ministry of the prophet Elijah to reconcile the hearts of the fathers to the children and the hearts of the children to the fathers. The idea is that through the end-time ministry of Elijah both the fathers and the children become of one heart and one mind!

Our Father in heaven wants children that are of Abraham, who is the father of the faithful. How can you be of Abraham if you do not have the same heart? We need to become of one heart and one mind with Abraham, our father!

Unfortunately, within Christianity at large there is a *"generation gap"* between the patriarchal fathers of the Bible and their children today. Why? Because, our biblical fathers' walked in obedience to the commandments given at Mount Sinai! Speaking of Abraham's example Our Creator said:

> *"For I have known him, in order that he may command his children and his household after him, that they keep the way of the LORD, to do righteousness and justice, that the LORD may bring to Abraham what He has spoken to him."*
>
> (Genesis 18:19)

WILL ABRAHAM
RECOGNIZE YOU?

The apostle Paul tells us:

> *"And if you are Christ's, then you are Abraham's seed, and heirs according to the promise."*
> (Galatians 3:29)

Children generally take on the characteristics, customs and the habits of their father's. We have a serious disconnect here, as the conduct of most Christians bears no relationship to that of Abraham. This is exactly what Messiah Yeshua talked about when He warned us with the following words:

> *"If you were Abraham's children you would do the works of Abraham."* (John 8:39b)

According to the prophet Isaiah, we are a rebellious people and *"Children who will not hear the law of the LORD."* (Isaiah 30:9) In this context, we can hardly expect Abraham to acknowledge us. He simply would not recognize most Christian believers today as his kin.

A TIME OF DECISION

If you are a practising Christian and have read this material, you are really facing the same choice Adam and Eve had to face in the Garden of Eden. The choice is as old as mankind. What is it to be? Will you chose the Tree of Life or the Tree of the Knowledge of Good and Evil? We all know they made the wrong choice with terrible consequences for mankind ever since that time. What are you going to do? Having come this far and having considered the Scriptures, it is now time to decide what to do. The question is; *'Are you going to follow the traditions of men or are you going to obey the commandments of God?'* On the one hand you have the established church saying that the Law has been done away and on the other the New Testament clearly and categorically states the opposite. Are you going by the traditions of your Church or are you going by the inspired and irrefutable word of God? We have here before us two opposing opinions and they cannot both be right.

What comes to mind is a Scripture from the Book of Kings where Elijah posed the following question:

> **"How long will you falter between two opinions?"** (1 Kings 18:21)

The choice then was to either follow God or to follow the false prophets of Baal. Having read this booklet, you face exactly the same choice today! It is a choice every bit as stark for you, as your choice too is to either follow God or continue in the false teaching of your church. In the Scriptures quoted in this booklet, you have been brought face to face with reality. What are you going to do? Which way are you going to go? John the Baptist went around preaching: *"**Repent, for the kingdom of heaven is at hand!**"* (Matthew 3:2)

To repent, literally means to turn around and go the other way into the opposite direction. The Hebrew word for repentance is full of meaning and it is pronounced *shoov.* The ancient meaning of the word is *'destroy the house.'* The word is composed of the Hebrew letters *'Sheen'* (שׁ) and *'Bet'* (ב). The letter *'Sheen,'* literally is teeth, it usually symbolises *'to destroy.'* The letter *'Bet,'* literally means *'a house.'* Real repentance occurs when we destroy the house. To repent means to destroy every last vestige of your old ungodly lifestyle. Real repentance is an all or nothing thing and it works because it is a complete break with the former self. To destroy the house, is to choose which kingdom and which covenant we will follow and to totally commit ourselves to that covenant. Jesus Himself, made a most pertinent comment about this matter of choice:

> *"**No man can serve two masters: for either he will hate the one, and love the other; or he will hold to the one, and despise the other.**"* (Luke 16:13)

If you have led a lawless life by accepting the delusion that the law has been done away, you are now at a crossroads in your life. You can either accept the word of God or you can simply reject it. God has made you a free moral agent and the choice is yours. Before I close, I would just like to quote you the most important words anyone could possibly ever hear. Yes, before we part company, just look at these awesome words from the mouth of your loving Creator:

> *"See, I have set before you today life and good, death and evil, in that I command you today to love the Lord your God, to walk in His ways, and to keep His commandments, His statutes, and His judgments, that you may live and multiply; and the Lord your God will bless you in the land which you go to possess."* (Deuteronomy 30:15-16)

Your loving Father in heaven then goes on to speak the words that come right out of the very core of His heart:

> *"I call heaven and earth as witnesses today against you, that as I have set before you life and death, blessing and cursing; THEREFORE CHOOSE LIFE, THAT BOTH YOU AND YOUR DESCENDANTS MAY LIVE."* (Deuteronomy 30:19)

If you wish to learn more and enter into true discipleship and to find out more about the authentic Hebrew roots of your faith, please feel free to contact:

BOOKS BY THE AUTHOR

ABOUT THE AUTHOR

STEPHEN J. SPYKERMAN, was born the fourth son of a Dutch father and an English mother in September 1940 during the Nazi occupation of Holland. The family escaped the Holocaust due to his parent's Catholic religion plus the fact that his mother was English and thus, she was seen as English rather than the Jewish woman. Stephen's early years were full of excitement and danger, as their house for some time became the emergency headquarters for the Dutch resistance in his region. His father was arrested by the Nazi authorities and held for some time in a special prison for people who were considered influential in their local communities. His parents also sheltered Henny Cohen, a Jewish woman, who was hiding whilst on the run from the Nazi's. At the same time their formidable children's nanny worked as a courier for the Dutch resistance.

Having received a solid general education, Stephen spurned the higher education his parents had hoped for and entered the world of retail fashion at the age of nineteen. He eventually left his hometown to try his luck in London, where he followed a generations old family tradition by becoming a tailor in a variety of high-class fashion houses. In 1965, he married Virginia Edwards. In time, he left the fashion industry and took up a more lucrative career in financial services. During his successful career, he pioneered a number of new schemes and concepts in charitable giving and seminar selling and became an international speaker in his field. His interest in public speaking led him to direct his own public speaking club. He, together with a colleague, he founded An International Speakers Bureau in London.

Stephen has a special interest in the State of Israel. He is a Member of the Temple Institute in Jerusalem and an Executive Associate of Kol Ha Tor, the Orthodox organization, which promotes reconciliation between the Two divided Houses of Israel. He is the Co-Founder of 'COI' - The Commonwealth Of Israel in Jerusalem, an organization whose purpose is to foster reconciliation between Ephraim, the so called Lost Tribes of the House of Israel and the House of Judah. Once retired from day to day business, he founded Mount Ephraim Publishing and started writing books and to this day continues to give lectures on his research. Stephen Spykerman has addressed audiences and conferences all over Europe, Israel and North America. *"Has the Law been Nailed to the Cross?"* is his first booklet.

Printed in Great Britain
by Amazon

54408930R00036